Prayer Before a Crucifix

Good and gentle Jesus,
here I kneel before you,
praying that you
will fill my heart with
faith, hope, and love.
I am truly sorry for my sins,
and I never want to do
wrong again.

I look at your five wounds
with love and sorrow,
and I remember what
your prophet, David,
said of you:

"They have pierced my
hands and my feet.
They have numbered
all my bones."

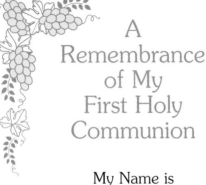

A Remembrance of My First Holy Communion

My Name is

_____

I Live at

_____

_____

I RECEIVED JESUS FOR THE FIRST TIME IN HOLY COMMUNION

in the Church of

_____

in the Town or City of

_____

on _____

Pastor

_____

My First Communion Book

Fr. Anthony A. Petrusic,
Consultant and Contributor

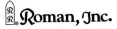
Roman, Inc.

Excerpts from the English translation of the
Roman Missal © 1985, International
Committee on English in the Liturgy, Inc. (ICEL);
and excerpts from the English translation of
the Eucharistic Prayers for Masses with Children
© 1975 ICEL.

Nihil Obstat
Sr. Marilyn Ellert, OSF
Censor deputatus

Imprimatur:
+ Bishop Joseph L. Imesch
Bishop of Joliet
May 21, 1999
Joliet, Illinois

Illustrations by Sue Shanahan

Designed by Anita M. Meyer

Writings and consultation by Fr. Anthony A.
Petrusic author of "Lift Up Your Hearts"

Published By Roman, Inc.
Roselle, Illinois • www.roman.com

Contents

Prayer Before a Crucifix..............3

To the Young Christian 11

My Daily Prayers 12

Your First Communion..............23

Order of the Mass 24

Communion Rite 53

Receiving Jesus in Communion..64

Sacrament of Reconciliation 67

My Life with Jesus in
Thought and Prayer 73

The Beatitudes 74

The Rosary 81

The Sacraments........................92

The Stations of the Cross..........95

The Life of Jesus 105

My Special Prayers..................120

To the Young Christian

This book has been written for you and for all those who wish to follow Jesus as good Christians.

To be like Jesus, we must love God with our whole heart and our neighbors as ourselves. That is not always easy, but with prayer and faith in God, it can be done. When praying, we talk to God and tell him of our needs as well as our thanks for his help.

The greatest prayer that Jesus left us is the Mass and we are called to take part in it every Sunday and sometimes more often. We are not alone anymore, He is with us as a friend and Savior.

My Daily Prayers

Jesus asks us to pray often every day so we can be his children and grow in his love. We begin by praying the Apostles' Creed in which we tell the world who we are and what we believe:

The Apostles' Creed

I believe in God, the Father almighty,
creator of heaven and earth.

I believe in Jesus Christ,
his only Son, our Lord.

He was conceived by the power of the
Holy Spirit and born of the Virgin Mary.

He suffered under Pontius Pilate,
was crucified, died, and was buried.

He descended to the dead.
On the third day he rose again.

He ascended into heaven, and is
seated at the right hand of the Father.

He will come again to judge
the living and the dead.

I believe in the Holy Spirit,
the holy catholic Church,
the communion of saints,
the forgiveness of sins,
the resurrection of the body,
and the life everlasting.

Amen.

The apostles who were special friends of Jesus asked him to teach them to pray. He gave them the Lord's Prayer:

The Lord's Prayer
(Our Father)

Our Father,
who art in heaven,
hallowed be thy name;
thy kingdom come;
thy will be done on
earth as it is in heaven.

Give us this day our daily
bread; and forgive us our
trespasses as we forgive
those who trespass against us;
and lead us not into
temptation, but deliver us
from evil.

Amen.

Jesus loved his mother, Mary, very much. When he was on the cross, He gave her to us to be our mother to whom we pray:

The Hail Mary

Hail Mary,
full of grace,
the Lord is with you.

Blessed are you
among women,
and blessed is the fruit
of your womb, Jesus.

Holy Mary,
Mother of God,
pray for us sinners,
now and at the hour
of our death.

Amen.

We always praise God in our prayers, especially this short one when we honor him as Father, Son and Holy Spirit:

Glory to the Father

**Glory to the Father,
and to the Son,
and to the Holy Spirit,
as it was in the
beginning, is now,
and will be for ever.
Amen.**

Morning Prayer

THE SIGN OF THE CROSS

In the name of the Father,
and of the Son,
and of the Holy Spirit.

Amen.

Lord Jesus, I am so glad that you
brought me to the beginning of a
new day.

I thank you very much and
I promise to do everything I can
to make it the best day of my life.

Protect and guard me from harm
and do not let me fall away from
you by sin.

Amen.

Prayer to My Guardian Angel

Angel of God, my guardian dear to whom God's love commits me here.

Ever this day be at my side to light and guide, to rule and guard me.

Amen.

As we learn to pray each day, how wonderful it is to turn to our heavenly Mother, Mary and ask her help. There is a beautiful poem by Mary Dixon Thayer which speaks to our hearts:

Lovely Lady
Dressed in Blue

Lovely Lady dressed in blue,
    teach me how to pray.
God was just your little boy,
    tell me what to say.
Did you lift him up sometimes,
    gently on your knee?
Did you sing to him the way
    mother does to me?
Did you hold his hand at night?
Did you ever try telling stories
    of the world?
O and did he cry?
Do you really think he'll care
    if I tell him things?
    little things that happen?
And do angels' wings make a noise?
And can he hear me if I speak low?
Does he understand me now?
Tell me, for you know!
Lovely Lady dressed in blue,
    teach me how to pray!
God was just your little boy,
    and you know the way!

Evening Prayers

Lord Jesus,
thank you for today.
It was your gift to me.

I tried to do the best I could.
Please accept it as my
gift back to you.

If I slipped away from your loving
arms, I ask your forgiveness.

Please, Lord Jesus, grant me a
peaceful night and restful sleep.

Bless my family and all those
who are close and good to me.

Give them your love and
protection. May we all ever
stay faithful to you.

Amen.

Now pray the Lord's Prayer, the Hail Mary and the Glory Be.

**Jesus meek and humble
of heart make my heart
be like yours.**

Your First Communion

When you were baptized you were called a child of God, and so indeed you are. Jesus took you to himself to be one with him. He loves you very much just as he loved his apostles and gave himself to them in the form of bread and wine....

"This is my body, this is my blood. Do this in memory of me."

The priest now continues to do the same thing at Mass so that Jesus again comes to us in Holy Communion.

You are a Catholic and a member of a big family of Jesus in his church. We all gather together to celebrate the Lord's supper at Mass. Jesus comes to us in the Eucharist, so we prepare by prayers and readings from the Bible. We praise him, and ask him to forgive our sins and grant us what we need. So we prepare to receive him in Holy Communion. Your best prayer at this time is to join in with the priests and people and respond to the prayers of the priest.

Order of the Mass

Introductory Rites

ENTRANCE SONG

(We stand.)

As the priest enters, we sing a song. Then we and the priest make the Sign of the Cross.

Priest: In the name of the Father, and of the Son, and of the Holy Spirit.

People: **Amen.**

GREETING

The priest greets us in the name of the Lord.

Priest: The grace of our Lord Jesus Christ and the love of God and the fellowship of the Holy Spirit be with you all.

People: **And also with you.**

Penitential Rite

The priest asks us to remember
our sins and to be sorry for them.
We do this in silence. Then we say
the following.

Priest and people:

I confess to almighty God, and to you, my brothers and sisters, that I have sinned through my own fault

(They strike their breast.)

in my thoughts and in my words, in what I have done and in what I have failed to do; and I ask blessed Mary, ever virgin, all the angels and saints, and you, my brothers and sisters, to pray for me to the Lord our God.

Priest:

May almighty God have mercy on us, forgive us our sins, and bring us to everlasting life.

People:

Amen.

Lord Have Mercy

If the Kyrie was not part of the Penitential Rite, it is said or sung by all. We say or sing the parts marked R.

V.	Lord, have mercy.
R.	**Lord, have mercy.**
V.	Christ, have mercy.
R.	**Christ, have mercy.**
V.	Lord, have mercy.
R.	**Lord, have mercy.**

Gloria

On most Sundays, this prayer of praise is said or sung:

Priest and people:

Glory to God in the highest, and peace to his people on earth. Lord God, heavenly King, almighty God and Father, we worship you, we give you thanks, we praise you for your glory. Lord Jesus Christ, only Son of the Father, Lord God, Lamb of God, you take away the sin of the world: have mercy on us; you are seated at the right hand of the Father: receive our prayer. For you alone are the Holy One, you alone are the Lord, you alone are the Most High, Jesus Christ, with the Holy Spirit, in the glory of God the Father.

Amen.

Opening Prayer

The priest prays to God our Father. We pray with him in silence.

Priest: Let us pray.

We pray silently.

The priest ends the prayer with:

Priest: ...for ever and ever.

People: **Amen.**

First Reading

(We sit.)

We listen to a reading from the old testament of the Bible.

Reader: The Word of the Lord.

People: **Thanks be to God.**

Responsorial Psalm

We repeat the response that is said or sung at the beginning. We say or sing it again after each verse. This prayer is taken from the book of Psalms in the Bible.

Second Reading

At the end we listen to a reading from the new testament of the Bible.

Reader: The Word of the Lord.

People: **Thanks be to God.**

(We stand.)

Gospel Acclamation

All repeat the Alleluia after the reader's Alleluia and again after the reader's verse.

Gospel

Deacon (or priest):
> The Lord be with you.

People: **And also with you.**

Deacon (or priest):
> A reading from the holy gospel according to N.

People: **Glory to you, Lord.**

(At the end:)

Deacon (or priest):
> The Gospel of the Lord.

People: **Praise to you, Lord Jesus Christ.**

Homily

(We sit.)

By reading from the Bible, the priest now explains what God has said to us. And by reading from the Gospels the priest explains about Jesus' teachings.

34

Profession of Faith

(We stand.)

We now say that we believe in God and in his Church.

We say this Profession of Faith together:

We believe in one God, the Father, the Almighty, maker of heaven and earth, of all that is seen and unseen.

We believe in one Lord, Jesus Christ, the only Son of God, eternally begotten of the Father, God from God, Light from Light, true God from true God, begotten, not made, one in Being with the Father.

Through him all things were made. For us men and for our salvation he came down from heaven:

(All bow at the following words up to: "and became man.")

by the power of the Holy Spirit he was born of the Virgin Mary, and became man.

For our sake he was crucified under Pontius Pilate; he suffered, died, and was buried.

On the third day he rose again in fulfillment of the Scriptures;

he ascended into heaven and is seated at the right hand of the Father.

He will come again in glory to judge the living and the dead, and his kingdom will have no end.

We believe in the Holy Spirit, the Lord, the giver of life, who proceeds from the Father and the Son.

With the Father and the Son he is worshiped and glorified.

He has spoken through the Prophets.

We believe in one holy catholic and apostolic Church.

We acknowledge one baptism for the forgiveness of sins.

We look for the resurrection of the dead, and the life of the world to come.

Amen.

(or, the Apostles' Creed may be said.)

Prayer of
the Faithful

We pray for the Church, for other people, and for our own needs. We listen to the prayers, and after each one we say:

People: **Lord, hear our prayer.**

At the end the priest says the concluding prayer and we say:

People: **Amen.**

(We sit.)

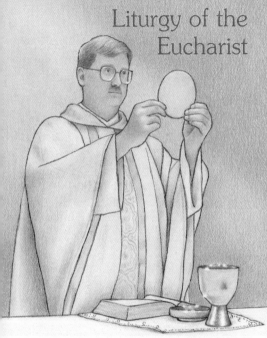

Liturgy of the Eucharist

In this part of the Mass, the bread and wine become the body and blood of Jesus. We shall receive him, and he will make us one with him and with all his people.

Preparation of the Altar and Gifts

Some of us carry the bread and wine to the priest.

Before the priest puts the bread on the altar, he says:

> Blessed are you, Lord, God of all creation. Through your goodness we have this bread to offer, which earth has given and human hands have made. It will become for us the bread of life.

People: **Blessed be God for ever.**

Before the priest places the chalice on the altar, he says:

> Blessed are you, Lord, God of all creation. Through your goodness we have this wine to offer, fruit of the vine and work of human hands. It will become our spiritual drink.

People: **Blessed be God for ever.**

Invitation to Prayer

Priest: Pray, my dear friends, that our sacrifice may be acceptable to God, the almighty Father.

People: **May the Lord accept the sacrifice at your hands for the praise and glory of his name, for our good and the good of all his Church.**

(We stand.)

Prayer over the Gifts

The priest, speaking in our name, asks the Father to bless and accept the gifts.

People: **Amen.**

Eucharistic Prayer

The central part of the Mass now begins. At the priest's invitation we lift our hearts to God and unite with him in the words he addresses to the Father through Jesus Christ.

Responding with the Priest's Invitation to Prayer

Priest: The Lord be with you.

People: **And also with you.**

Priest: Lift up your hearts.

People: **We lift them up to the Lord.**

Priest: Let us give thanks to the Lord our God.

People: **It is right to give him thanks and praise.**

Preface of the Mass

Father, it is our duty and our salvation, always and everywhere to give you thanks through your beloved Son, Jesus Christ.

He is the Word through whom you made the universe, the Savior you sent to redeem us.

By the power of the Holy Spirit he took flesh and was born of the Virgin Mary.

For our sake he opened his arms on the cross; he put an end to death and revealed the resurrection.

In this he fulfilled your will and won for you a holy people.

And so we join the angels and the saints in proclaiming your glory as we sing (say):

Acclamation

Priest and people:

Holy, holy, holy Lord,
God of power and might,
heaven and earth are full
of your glory.
Hosanna in the highest.
Blessed is he who comes
in the name of the Lord.
Hosanna in the highest.

(We kneel.)

Eucharistic Prayer

There are several different Eucharistic prayers which the priest may use. An example is the one which follows, Eucharistic Prayer number two. Whichever prayer is used, we listen and pray in silence until we are called upon to respond.

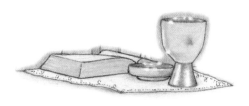

Eucharistic Prayer for Children, II

Priest:

God, our loving Father, we are glad to give you thanks and praise because you love us. With Jesus we sing your praise:

Priest and people:

Glory to God in the highest.

Priest:

Because you love us, you gave us this great and beautiful world. With Jesus we sing your praise:

Priest and people:

Glory to God in the highest.

Priest:

Because you love us, you sent Jesus your Son to bring us to you and to gather us around him as the children of one family. With Jesus we sing your praise:

Priest and people:

Glory to God in the highest.

Priest:

For such great love, we thank you with the angels and saints as they praise you and sing (say):

Priest and people:

Holy, holy, holy Lord,
God of power and might,
heaven and earth are full
of your glory.
Hosanna in the highest.

Blessed is he who comes
in the name of the Lord.
Hosanna in the highest.

Priest:

Blessed be Jesus, whom you sent to be the friend of children and of the poor. He came to show us how we can love you, Father, by loving one another.

He came to take away sin, which keeps us from being friends, and hate, which makes us all unhappy.

He promised to send the Holy Spirit, to be with us always so that we can live as your children.

Priest and people:

Blessed is he who comes in the name of the Lord. Hosanna in the highest.

Priest:

God our Father, we now ask you to send your Holy Spirit to change these gifts of bread and wine into the body and blood of Jesus Christ, our Lord.

The night before he died, Jesus your Son showed us how much you love us. When he was at supper with his disciples, he took bread, and gave you thanks and praise. Then he broke the bread, gave it to his friends, and said:

Take this, all of you, and eat it: This is my body which will be given up for you.

Priest and people:
Jesus has given his life for us.

Priest:
When supper was ended, Jesus took the cup that was filled with wine. He thanked you, gave it to his friends, and said:

Take this, all of you, and drink from it: this is the cup of my blood, the blood of the new and everlasting covenant. It will be shed for you and for all so that sins may be forgiven.

Priest and people:

Jesus has given his life for us.

Priest:

Then he said to them:
Do this in memory of me.
And so, loving Father, we
remember that Jesus died and
rose again to save the world.
He put himself into our hands to
be the sacrifice we offer you.

Priest and people:

We praise you, we bless you, we
thank you.

Priest:

Lord our God listen to our prayer.
Send the Holy Spirit to all of us
who share in this meal. May this
Spirit bring us closer together
in the family of the Church, with
N., our pope, N., our bishop, all
other bishops, and all who serve
your people.

Priest and people:
We praise you, we bless you, we thank you.

Priest:
Remember, Father, our families and friends and all those we do not love as we should. Remember those who have died. Bring them home to you to be with you for ever.

Priest and people:
We praise you, we bless you, we thank you.

Priest:
Gather us all together into your kingdom. There we shall be happy for ever with the Virgin Mary, Mother of God and our mother. There all the friends of Jesus the Lord will sing a song of joy.

Priest and people:

We praise you, we bless you, we thank you.

Priest:

Through him, with him, in him, in the unity of the Holy Spirit, all glory and honor is yours, almighty Father for ever and ever.

Priest and people respond:

Amen.

Communion Rite

Lord's Prayer

(We stand.)

Priest: Let us pray with confidence
to the Father in the words
our Savior gave us:

Priest and people:

Our Father, who art in heaven,
hallowed be thy name;
thy kingdom come;
thy will be done on earth
as it is in heaven.

Give us this day our daily bread;
and forgive us our trespasses
as we forgive those who
trespass against us; and lead
us not into temptation, but
deliver us from evil.

Priest:

Deliver us, Lord, from every evil,
and grant us peace in our day.

In your mercy keep us free from
sin and protect us from all anxiety
as we wait in joyful hope for the
coming of our Savior, Jesus Christ.

People:

For the kingdom, the power,
and the glory are yours,
now and for ever.

Sign of Peace

Sign of Peace

The priest says the prayer for peace:

> Lord Jesus Christ, you said
> to your apostles: "I leave
> you peace, my peace I give
> you. Look not on our sins,
> but on the faith of your
> Church, and grant us the
> peace and unity of your
> kingdom where you live
> for ever and ever."

People: **Amen.**

Priest: The peace of the Lord be
with you always.

People: **And also with you.**

Deacon (or priest):
> Let us offer each other the
> sign of peace.

We wish each other peace, to show
our love.

Breaking of
the Bread

The priest breaks the bread and drops a piece of it into the chalice. During the breaking of the bread, we pray or sing:

**Lamb of God,
you take away
the sins of the world:
have mercy on us.**

**Lamb of God,
you take away
the sins of the world:
have mercy on us.**

**Lamb of God,
you take away
the sins of the world:
grant us peace.**

Preparation for Communion

The priest quietly says a prayer:

Lord Jesus Christ,
Son of the living God,
by the will of the Father
and the work of the
Holy Spirit your death
brought life to the world.

By your holy body and blood
free me from all my sins
and from every evil.

Keep me faithful to your
teaching, and never let me
be parted from you.

Communion

Priest: This is the Lamb of God who takes away the sins of the world. Happy are those who are called to his supper.

Priest and people:
Lord, I am not worthy to receive you, but only say the word and I shall be healed.

Before receiving communion, the priest says quietly:

May the body of Christ bring me to everlasting life, and may the blood of Christ bring me to everlasting life.

The priest then gives communion to the people.

Priest: The body of Christ.

Communicant: **Amen.**

Priest: The blood of Christ.

Communicant: **Amen.**

Communion Song

Silence after Communion

(We sit.)

After communion we pray silently, or we may sing a hymn of praise.

Prayer after Communion

(We stand.)

Priest: Let us pray.

Priest and people may pray silently for a while. Then the priest says the Prayer after Communion.

At the end of this Prayer, the priest says:

> We ask this through
> Christ our Lord.

People: **Amen.**

Concluding Rite

After any brief announcements the blessing and dismissal follow:

Priest: The Lord be with you.

People: **And also with you.**

Blessing

Priest: May almighty God bless you, the Father, and the Son, and the Holy Spirit.

People: **Amen.**

Dismissal

Deacon (or priest):

Go in peace to love and serve the Lord.

People: **Thanks be to God.**

Receiving
Jesus in
Communion

The Eucharist

When we go to Mass to celebrate the Eucharist, we receive Jesus who loved children and called them to himself. He calls us now, especially at First Communion and ever after.

The priest or minister holds up the host and says, "The Body of Christ" and you respond "Amen".

The priest or minister holds up the cup and says, "The Blood of Christ" and you respond "Amen".

"Amen" means that I believe this is truly the Body and Blood of Jesus."

As you return to your seat, pause for a silent moment to thank Jesus for coming to you.

Some Things
to Remember

We do not eat anything for an hour before Communion. But we may take medicine and water during that time. Communion is a great gift from God. That is why so many boys and girls go to Mass and Communion on weekdays. They receive our Lord on holidays, on Saturdays, and during vacation. Perhaps you can, too.

Sacrament of
Reconciliation

Getting Ready
to Reconcile

Jesus loves us so much, but there are times we forget to be faithful to him. We do things which we should not and commit sins by hurting others and forgetting our prayers and respect for God. Jesus calls us back so we can be forgiven just as he always forgave those with sins who came to him. Now you go to the priest, confess your sins and he forgives you in the name of Jesus. You tell Jesus that you are sorry for offending him and promise to do better in the future.

Before going before the priest for reconciliation, spend some time in prayer and thought about what sins you may have committed and for which you ask forgiveness:

DO I SHOW MY LOVE FOR GOD?

Do I talk to God every day in prayer, and listen to him?

Do I go to Mass on Sundays? Am I quiet and respectful in church?

Do I say the names "God" and "Jesus" with respect?

DO I DO MY DUTY?

Do I try to do my best in school?

Do I help my parents at home?

Do I take care of my body?

How Do I Act with Others?

Do I talk kindly to other people?

Do I share my things with others?

Do I always tell the truth?

Do I ever take things that are not mine?

Do I ever make fun of others?

Do I treat my parents and teachers with respect?

Upon entering the reconciliation room or confessional, you go before the priest who welcomes you and together you make the Sign of the Cross.

We Now Tell Our Sins

The priest talks to us and tries to help us and answer our questions as well as give us advice. Then he gives a penance which we must pray or do after we leave the place of reconciliation.

Now you listen for The Prayer of Forgiveness.

We Are Forgiven

The priest then forgives our sins in God's name.

Priest:

God, the Father of mercies,
through the death and resurrection
of his Son has reconciled the
world to himself and sent
the Holy Spirit among us for the
forgiveness of sins; through
the ministry of the Church may
God give you pardon and peace,
and I absolve you from your sins in
the name of the Father, and
of the Son, and of the Holy Spirit.

We say: **Amen.**

Priest: Give thanks to the Lord for
he is good.

We say: **His mercy endures for ever.**

Pray Your
Act of Contrition

My God, I am sorry for my sins
    with all my heart.
In choosing to do wrong and
    failing to do good,
I have sinned against you whom
    I should love above all things.
I firmly intend, with your help,
    to do penance, to sin no more,
and to avoid whatever leads me
    to sin.
Our Savior Jesus Christ suffered
    and died for us.
In his name, my God have Mercy.

The priest now will tell you to leave
and go in peace and you respond:

"Thanks be to God."

My Life
with Jesus in
Thought and Prayer

The Beatitudes

When Jesus gathered his disciples, a very large crowd of people came along to a hillside to hear him. Jesus said if they wanted to be his followers and reach heaven they should follow his Beatitudes or guidelines. They are:

BLESSED ARE THE POOR IN SPIRIT, FOR THEIRS IS THE KINGDOM OF HEAVEN.

We pray: Lord, teach me to place my trust in you and not only in the possessions I may have.

BLESSED ARE THEY WHO MOURN, FOR THEY SHALL BE COMFORTED.

We pray: Lord, we are weak human beings who sometimes are hurt and very sad. Help us to lift up our hearts to you to receive the comfort which only you can give.

BLESSED ARE THE MEEK, FOR THEY SHALL INHERIT THE LAND.

We pray: Lord, grant me the grace to have genuine meekness and humility. You are the source of all we are and all we have. By serving you we will inherit your promise.

BLESSED ARE THEY WHO HUNGER AND THIRST FOR HOLINESS, FOR THEY WILL BE SATISFIED.

We pray: Lord, may I ever strive to be holy and to live according to your holy will. Never let me be separated from you by sin and neglect.

BLESSED ARE THE MERCIFUL, FOR MERCY WILL BE SHOWN TO THEM.

We pray: Lord, I pray for the strength to show kindness to others, especially the poor, those suffering and the lonely. Even the little good deeds we do will not go unrewarded.

BLESSED ARE THE CLEAN OF HEART, FOR THEY WILL SEE GOD.

We pray: Lord, help me to always keep my heart and body clean and free from temptation and sin. I wish to be yours and to finally reach the eternal goal of seeing you face to face.

BLESSED ARE THE PEACEMAKERS, FOR THEY SHALL BE CALLED CHILDREN OF GOD

We pray: Lord, there are so many opportunities to be a peacemaker at home, in school and with my friends. I want to be a Child of God. Help me to stand strong when I am faced with a decision for peace.

BLESSED ARE THEY WHO ARE PERSECUTED FOR HOLINESS SAKE, FOR THEIRS IS THE KINGDOM OF HEAVEN.

We pray: Lord, may I always be a faithful witness to you and your holy law. Do not let me abandon you, even when the going gets tough. The road to your kingdom is not always easy, but with your help I can stay on it and finally reach the promised land.

Jesus Loves Us and Asks Our Love in Return

When Jesus talked to the crowds of people around him, they asked what the greatest commandment might be. He replied:

You must love God above all things and love your neighbor as yourself.

How do we do that? Jesus said we love him when we keep his commandments, the ten commandments God gave to Moses a long time ago.

The first three commandments show us how to love God:

1. I am the Lord your God and you should not have strange gods before me.
2. You should not take the name of the Lord in vain.
3. You must keep holy the Lord's Day.

The last seven commandments show us how to love our neighbor:

4. Honor your father and your mother.

5. You should not kill.

6. Do not commit adultery.

7. You should not steal.

8. You should not bear false witness against your neighbor.

9. You should not covet your neighbor's wife.

10. You should not covet your neighbor's goods.

Jesus tells us that if we keep his commandments, we shall live and be his children. He also tells us to pray always. It is wonderful to pray to Mary his mother and with her learn more about his life and love for us.

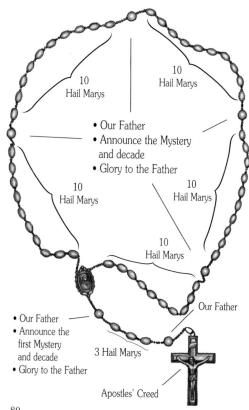

10
Hail Marys

10
Hail Marys

- Our Father
- Announce the Mystery and decade
- Glory to the Father

10
Hail Marys

10
Hail Marys

10
Hail Marys

Our Father

- Our Father
- Announce the first Mystery and decade
- Glory to the Father

3 Hail Marys

Apostles' Creed

The Rosary

The Rosary is a way of talking to Mary, the Mother of Jesus, and our Blessed Mother. It is a way of praising her. It is a way of asking her to pray for us, her children.

The Rosary is divided into groups or decades, of ten small beads. Before each decade there is one big bead. On the big bead, we say an Our Father. On each small bead we say a Hail Mary. At the end of each decade, we say the Glory to the Father.

As we say a decade, we think of something that happened to our Blessed Mother or Jesus. The first five decades are called the Joyful Mysteries. The second five decades are the Sorrowful Mysteries. The third five decades are the Glorious Mysteries.

The First Joyful Mystery

THE ANNUNCIATION

The angel tells Mary that she will be the Mother of Jesus. Mary answers that she will do whatever God asks of her.

I shall try to be like Mary. I shall try to do whatever God asks of me.

The Second Joyful Mystery

THE VISITATION

Mary goes to visit her cousin Elizabeth, who needs help. Elizabeth is happy to see Mary and talk with her.

Like Mary, I shall try to help my family and friends.

The Third Joyful Mystery

THE BIRTH OF JESUS

Mary laid Jesus in a manger because there was no room for them at the inn.

God loves the poor and the weak. I shall love them, too.

The Fourth Joyful Mystery

THE PRESENTATION OF JESUS IN THE TEMPLE

Mary and Joseph obeyed the law and took Jesus to the Temple. There they presented him to the Lord.

I, too, shall obey God's law. I shall obey all those he has placed over me.

The Fifth Joyful Mystery

THE FINDING OF JESUS IN THE TEMPLE

The boy Jesus was lost. But after a long search, Mary and Joseph found him in the Temple.

I know where to find Jesus. He is with the people I meet every day. When I am kind to them, I am kind to Jesus.

The First
Sorrowful Mystery

THE SUFFERINGS OF JESUS IN
THE GARDEN OF GETHSEMANE

In the garden, Jesus asked God to take away his sufferings. But Jesus wanted, above all, to do his Father's will.

I, too, want to do the will of God, even when he asks for something that is hard.

The Second
Sorrowful Mystery

THE SCOURGING OF JESUS

Jesus' friends ran away from him and left him alone. Then Pilate had Jesus tied to a pillar, and soldiers whipped him.

I shall be friendly with boys and girls who are alone and lonely.

The Third
Sorrowful Mystery

THE CROWNING WITH THORNS

The Roman soldiers put a crown of thorns on Jesus' head. Then they made fun of him.

I shall remember how the soldiers treated Jesus. I shall never hurt or make fun of anyone.

The Fourth
Sorrowful Mystery

THE CARRYING OF THE CROSS

Jesus carried his cross to a hill called Calvary. There the soldiers nailed him to the cross.

Sometimes I must do things I don't enjoy. Then I remember Jesus carrying that heavy cross up the hill of Calvary.

The Fifth
Sorrowful Mystery

THE DEATH OF JESUS ON THE CROSS

Jesus hung on the cross three hours. Then he spoke to his Father in heaven and died.

Jesus died for every one of us, even those people I find it hard to like. I shall try to love them because Jesus gave up his life for them.

The First
Glorious Mystery

THE RESURRECTION OF JESUS

Jesus died on Good Friday. He rose again on Easter.

I rose with Jesus when I was baptized. Now I shall try to be a good follower of our Lord and a good Christian.

The Second
Glorious Mystery

THE ASCENSION OF JESUS

While the Apostles watched, Jesus ascended into heaven and could no longer be seen.

Although I cannot see Jesus, I am able to receive him in Holy Communion every day.

The Third
Glorious Mystery

THE COMING OF THE HOLY SPIRIT

The Apostles met in a big room. Suddenly they heard a noise like the wind, and they were all filled with the Holy Spirit. At once they went out and preached about Jesus.

I am not big enough to preach, but I can act like a follower of Jesus. The people who see me will know how a true Christian acts.

The Fourth
Glorious Mystery

THE ASSUMPTION OF OUR
BLESSED MOTHER INTO HEAVEN

Mary, the Mother of Jesus, was taken into heaven.

I ask our Blessed Mother to help me and those I love, for she is in heaven with her son Jesus.

The Fifth
Glorious Mystery

THE CROWNING OF OUR
BLESSED MOTHER AS QUEEN OF
HEAVEN AND EARTH

In heaven, our Blessed Mother was made Queen of Heaven and Earth.

Mary, Queen of Heaven, is the mother of us all. I ask her to pray that we, her children, may have peace in our families, in our country, and in every place on earth.

The Sacraments

Christ established seven sacraments which are visible signs of God's grace on us. These sacraments are entrusted to the church and are given at special moments in a person's life and are important parts of our Christian faith.

SACRAMENTS OF INITIATION

Baptism

Our first sacrament is baptism or christening. Baptism initiates us as members of the church. As we are baptized, it is said:

I baptize you in the name of the Father, the Son, and the Holy Spirit. Amen.

Confirmation

When we are confirmed, we receive the mark of the Holy Spirit which lets us lead a spiritual life as Jesus would have us live our lives.

Eucharist

Eucharist is Communion, a sacrament during which we receive Christ in the form of the consecrated bread which is his body, and consecrated wine which is his blood. Christ is always with us.

SACRAMENTS OF HEALING

Reconciliation

The sacrament of Reconciliation allows us to become holy by being forgiven by God. It reconciles us with God and with the Church.

Anointing of the Sick

For those who are very old or seriously sick, this sacrament prepares those who suffer for heaven by increasing God's grace, sanctifying the sufferings and forgiving all sins.

SACRAMENTS AT THE SERVICE OF COMMUNION

Holy Orders

The Holy Orders gives priests and bishops the powers of grace and guidance to forgive sins, anoint the sick, change the bread and wine to the body and blood of Christ and to perform Mass which represents Christ's sacrifices for us.

Matrimony

The sacrament of matrimony is given by the husband and wife to each other as they pronounce their marriage vows. Matrimony gives the grace to both to join their lives together until death. The priest is the church witness of the giving of this sacrament.

The
Stations
of the
Cross

Each Station of the Cross shows us what Jesus went through on his journey to Calvary where he would die so that we might be saved and live.

When we pray the Stations of the Cross in church and pause in front of the picture or statue on the wall, we pray and think of what Jesus did for our sake.

Before you begin the Stations, kneel and pray:

Jesus, you loved me so much that you died for my sins and rose again so I might share in eternal life with you, the Father and the Holy Spirit. May these Stations of the Cross help me to realize that love.

At each station pray:
  one Our Father,
  one Hail Mary and
  one Glory to the Father.

First Station

My Lord, Jesus,
help me to ever
stand by you
and do what
you want of me.
I will never
abandon you.

Jesus is Condemned to Death

Second Station

My Lord, Jesus,
when things don't
go my way I like
to complain.
Help me to
remember what
you did for me
when you took
the heavy cross
upon your shoulders.

Jesus Takes Up His Cross

Third Station

My Lord, Jesus, I fall many times when I do not do what is right. Lift me up and keep me close to your heart so I may be safe.

Jesus Falls for the First Time

Fourth Station

My Lord, Jesus, your mother Mary was there to comfort you on this sad journey to Calvary. Mary, help me to stay close to your son always.

Jesus Meets His Mother

Fifth Station

My Lord, Jesus, how wonderful of Simon to take your cross and help you. May I learn to help others always.

Simon of Cyrene Helps Jesus

Sixth Station

My Lord, Jesus, Veronica did not hang back when there was something good to be done. She bravely reached through the crowd and wiped your sore face. Let me reach out each day as well to help someone.

Veronica Wipes Jesus' Face

Seventh Station

My Lord, Jesus,
you fall a second
time and your
cross gets heavier.
Let me not stumble
when my little
crosses seem too heavy.
You are within me.

Jesus Falls a Second Time

Eighth Station

My Lord, Jesus, in
the midst of your
suffering and agony,
you took time to
comfort the good
women from
Jerusalem who came
to comfort you.
Thank you for all
that you do for us with
your grace and comfort.

Jesus Meets the Sorrowing Women

Ninth Station

My Lord, Jesus, this third fall must have been extra hard on your weakened body. You rose, however, to reach the hill of Calvary. Lift me up and make me strong against all temptation and sin.

Jesus Falls a Third Time

Tenth Station

My Lord, Jesus, I regret so much that sins of those who you are going to die to save, now make you an object of shame. Keep me strong and pure always as I see what you did for me.

Jesus' Clothes are Torn from Him

Eleventh Station

My Lord, Jesus,
how much pain
you already endured
and now the worst,
being nailed to the
Cross. Your love
for us is so great,
may I love you in return.

Jesus is Nailed to the Cross

Twelfth Station

(please kneel.)

My Lord, Jesus,
thank you for this
great sacrifice you
made for us. Do
not let me ever
be separated from
you by sin or neglect.
Stay close to me all
the days of my life.

Jesus Dies on the Cross

Thirteenth Station

My Lord, Jesus, as your body was taken down from the cross and placed in the arms of your mother, Mary, we realize how sad that moment must have been. You gave Mary to all of us before you died to be our mother. May we always love and be faithful to her call.

Jesus is Placed in Mary's Arms

Fourteenth Station

My Lord, Jesus, we know that this is not the end as many thought. Three days later you will rise from the grave and conquer death once and for all. You give us great hope. Thank you, my beloved Savior.

Jesus is Laid in the Tomb

Jesus Rises from the Dead

Fifteenth Station

(before the altar)

My Lord, Jesus, how wonderful it was when your friends would see you alive. Your body still had the marks of death, but now they shone as marks of victory. I praise you and wish to love you always.

The Life of Jesus

THE BIRTH OF JESUS

Long ago, in the town of Nazareth, an angel of the Lord spoke with a young woman named Mary who was engaged to Joseph, a carpenter.

The angel told Mary that she would become the mother of a child named Jesus who would be called the Son of God. Young Mary replied to the angel that she would do all that God had asked of her.

As time grew near for the birth of the child, Mary and her husband Joseph traveled far across the desert to the little town of Bethlehem.

Late at night, Mary and Joseph arrived in Bethlehem. The town was very crowded so they were given shelter in a small stable which they shared with sheep, cattle and donkeys.

In the tiny stable, Mary gave birth to Jesus, the Son of God. The angels of heaven rejoiced and spread the word to shepherds and wise men that unto all a King, the Son of God, had been born.

A brilliant star appeared in the heavens and the angels told the wise men to follow the star to the stable in Bethlehem so that they could see the newborn King.

The wise men honored Jesus with gifts of frankincense, gold and myrrh, because when they saw him, they knew that he was the King who would be a Savior of all.

The shepherds and wise men soon went on their way and told of the birth of Jesus to everyone they met. Soon the good news of the birth of our Savior was known by people near and far.

THE FLIGHT INTO EGYPT

When King Herod learned of the birth of Jesus he became angry because he believed that he should be the only King for his people. He tried to find Jesus by sending his soldiers and servants out among the people.

An angel from God told Joseph and Mary to take Jesus to another land called Egypt. So Jesus, Mary and Joseph traveled to Egypt and remained safe from the danger of King Herod.

JESUS AT THE TEMPLE

When Joseph and Mary returned to Nazareth with the baby Jesus, they presented him to God at the temple and named him Jesus.

At the temple, Jesus was recognized by people such as Simeon and Anna and they spread the word that our Savior had come.

Jesus spent his childhood in Nazareth and from his father learned well how to do the work of a fine carpenter.

Jesus studied and learned of the meaning and way of God's holy word. He became known as kind and obedient to God's word.

When Jesus was twelve years old, he went to Jerusalem with his parents to celebrate a holiday. When the holiday ended, Joseph and Mary were traveling home when they found that Jesus was not with them. So they went back to Jerusalem and found that Jesus was at the temple and was talking with teachers and friends about the word of God.

When Joseph and Mary asked Jesus why he had stayed in Jerusalem and had worried them, he explained to them that he must do his Father's work.

THE APOSTLES AND FOLLOWERS OF JESUS

People who heard of Jesus' teachings came from places far away to learn of God's word and to learn how to pray. Many learned of God's love for us and how to show their love for God.

Jesus started to travel about and tell of God's great love to many people. At this time, Jesus was thirty years old.

During his travels, he met those who became his apostles such as the two brothers Peter and Andrew and the brothers James and John. When he met them and talked with them, he asked these brothers to follow him and help to spread the word of God. These brothers left their work and families behind and followed Jesus to help him tell people about the love of God.

As many people learned of God's love, they followed him and also helped him to spread the word of God. Of these many people, Jesus chose twelve men to be his apostles. As these apostles traveled with him, he taught them all about God's ways and let them know that their job was to help to teach about God to the whole world.

While meeting people and speaking to them, Jesus taught them many things such as the Lord's prayer and how to keep the commandments of the Lord.

ONE OF JESUS' MIRACLES

At one time during his travels, Jesus spoke of the word of God to five thousand people as he sat on a hillside in the hot sun. The people listened to him for over five hours.

Jesus knew that many of the people had traveled for quite a distance to listen to him and that they did not have food to eat or water to drink before they traveled home.

He asked that his apostles go to find food and drink so that followers could have what they needed. The apostles could find only a boy who carried five loaves of bread and two fish.

Jesus asked the apostles to give the small amount of bread and fish to the five thousand people. To their surprise the two fish and five loaves of bread became enough to feed the 5,000 people as much as they wanted. It was soon realized that Jesus had performed a miracle and that the miracle was an example of Jesus' love. And, Jesus let it be known that the miracle was from the power of God.

During his travels and while teaching about the word of God, Jesus accomplished many miracles which relieved many people of their sufferings such as being blind, crippled or very sick. Each time a miracle was performed, the people learned to understand the love and power of God.

JESUS ENTERS JERUSALEM

As Jesus spoke to people and they gained an understanding of God's word, they too spread the lessons learned and so the number of friends and followers of Jesus grew. And, many traveled with him as he continued his mission.

A large crowd of followers and friends greeted Jesus as he entered the town of Jerusalem and proclaimed him as the Son of God.

But, as the crowd of followers grew there were those who did not believe his teachings and became angry. Those who were angry and who had power made plans to keep their own power by arresting Jesus for claiming that he was the Son of God. They wanted people to honor them as rulers and kings and not to believe in Jesus.

THE LAST SUPPER

During the Last Supper with his apostles, Jesus knew that they were afraid for him. He calmed their fears, gave them bread and said,

"Take this and eat; it is my body."

Then he gave them a cup of wine and said,

"Drink this; it is my blood."

Jesus also told them, "Love one another as I love you. Soon I will leave you and go to my Father. But I will send the Holy Spirit who will live with you and teach you what you need to know."

JESUS DIED SO THAT OUR SINS WOULD BE FORGIVEN

Jesus was then arrested by those who had power and did not believe that he was the Son of God. He did not deny that he was the Son of God and so he gave his life so that our sins would be forgiven.

Jesus' followers and friends knew that he would be taken to Calvary and would be crucified. He spoke to his friends and let them know that he would rise in three days.

While hanging on the cross on Calvary, Jesus asked God to forgive those who had harmed him because they did not know what they had done.

JESUS RISES

Jesus was buried in the tomb and after three days, it was found that the tomb was empty. And they were told that Jesus had risen.

Jesus then visited his apostles so that they could see that he had risen and asked that they teach the people what he had been able to teach them. For us Jesus made the sacrifice of giving up his life and then came back from the dead. This has shown us the power of God's love. We also know that our love for God allows us to have life with him forever.

My Special Prayers

A PRAYER FOR PERSEVERANCE AND LIGHT

Dear Lord, Jesus,
I love you with all of my heart and I
wish to stay faithful to you. I ask for the
strength to remain with you in all things
and ask that your holy will be done.

Keep me safe from sin and all
that is evil. May I ever be an example to
others by the way I live, act and speak.

May your Holy Spirit guide my steps
as I advance in age, grace and wisdom.

Teach me to do your will and to follow
the path of life you have destined for me.

If it is your will that I am called to
the priesthood or religious life, give me
the courage and perseverance to
follow that calling.

Whatever your calling for me is, dear
Lord, may I always do my best to follow
in your footsteps and praise and
thank you for it all.   Amen.

A Prayer for Family

Dear Jesus, I ask your blessing and protection on my family each and every day.

May we live in peace and with love for you and one another. I pray that no harm befall us and that good health, happiness and blessings from above will always be with us.

May your Mother Mary and St. Joseph be a model for us as was your Holy Family home in Nazareth.

Amen.

Prayer for Peace of St. Francis

Lord, make me an instrument
of your peace.
Where there is hatred…
let me sow love.
Where is injury…pardon.
Where there is doubt…faith.
Where there is despair…hope.
Where there is darkness…light.
Where there is sadness…joy.

O Divine Master,
grant that I may not so much seek
to be consoled as to console,
to be understood as to understand,
to be loved as to love.

For
It is in giving that we receive,
it is in pardoning
that we are pardoned,
it is in dying that we are born
to eternal life.

I Said a Prayer
for You Today

I said a prayer for you today
I know that God must have heard.

I felt the answer in my heart
although he spoke no word.

I didn't ask for wealth or fame.
(I knew you wouldn't mind.)

I asked him to send treasures
of a far more lasting kind.

I prayed that he would be near you
at the start of each new day,
to grant you health and blessings
and friends to share your way.

I asked for happiness for you
in all things great and small.

But it was for his loving care
I prayed for most of all.

My Personal Record

Name_____

    Born_____in_____

Baptism   Date_____

    Priest_____

    Parish_____

    Godmother_____

    Godfather_____

First Communion Date_____

    Priest_____

    Parish_____

Confirmation   Date_____

    Priest_____

    Sponsor_____

    Confirmation
    Name_____

My Thoughts and What I Have Learned

_____

_____
_____
_____
_____
_____
_____
_____
_____
_____
_____
_____
_____
_____
_____
_____
_____
_____
_____
_____
_____

My Thoughts and What I Have Learned